T3-ATO-994

# GREATEST MOVIE MONSTERS™

# ZOMBIES

KATHRYN MORGAN

Published in 2016 by The Rosen Publishing Group, Inc.
29 East 21st Street, New York, NY 10010

First Edition

**Library of Congress Cataloging-in-Publication Data**

Morgan, Kathryn, 1983– author.
Zombies/Kathryn Morgan.—First edition.
     pages cm.—(Greatest movie monsters)
Includes bibliographical references and index.
Includes filmography.
ISBN 978-1-4994-3545-0 (library bound) — ISBN 978-1-4994-3547-4 (pbk.) — ISBN 978-1-4994-3548-1 (6-pack)
1. Zombie films—History—Juvenile literature. 2. Zombies—Folklore—
Juvenile literature. I. Title.
PN1995.9.Z63M67 2016
791.43'67—dc23

2014045480

*Manufactured in the United States of America*

**On the cover:** 2010 promotional poster for the popular AMC television series *The Walking Dead.*

# THE ORIGINS OF ZOMBIES

Legends of the dead returning to walk the earth have frightened and fascinated people for centuries. Yet, not all undead are created equal. Vampires and other monsters, such as Frankenstein, are examples of the risen dead that are not classified as zombies. So what makes a zombie? The word *zombie* entered the English language thanks to Robert Southey's novel *A History of Brazil*, published in 1819. Southey used this word, which was spelled "zombi," to describe mindless, reanimated corpses. Unlike the brain-hungry monstrosities that movies today promote, originally zombies were always said to be fairly tame.

Zombies have captivated the imaginations of people everywhere. These undead creations have become a common feature in novels, video games, comics, and the film industry—often as an ideal villain. So where did stories of such gruesome creations originate? Many people do not realize that zombie legends have their origins in Haiti or that the zombies of past lore vary widely from the zombies shown in modern films.

*The popular television show* **The Walking Dead** *portrays the typical contemporary depiction of zombies rather than following the descriptions of traditional zombie folklore.*

## THE ORIGINS OF THE UNDEAD

Haiti occupies a portion slightly smaller than the size of Maryland on the island of Hispaniola in the Caribbean Sea. At one time, forests covered a majority of the country, but today Haiti primarily consists of farmland. While Haitians are entitled to religious freedom, the majority practice either Roman Catholicism, Vodou, or a blend of practices and beliefs taken from both. It is from the Vodou religion (which is related to what is commonly called "voodoo" as well as to the West African religion Vodun) that we get the idea of the zombie.

Because of the widespread influence of Vodou, Haitian culture has numerous tales of these bodies that are brought back to life by a *bokor*, or Vodou sorcerer. Unlike many of the zombies we see in movies today, these reanimated bodies were not said to be particularly dangerous. Instead, the Haitian zombie was a mindless slave that belonged to and obeyed the *bokor* who had brought it back from the grave. The word *zombie* itself even means

*This 1595 engraving depicts African slaves performing various agricultural tasks on a Haitian plantation. Early Haitian depictions of zombies resembled the conditions of poorly treated, enslaved workers.*

"spirit of the dead" in certain African languages that influenced Haitian Creole—the language spoken in Haiti. A zombie was the result of when a *bokor* removed and took possession of a victim's soul. Sometimes this process began while the victim was still alive; in other stories, it occurred entirely after death. Many times, zombification was sometimes viewed as a punishment for those who had wronged the *bokor* in his or her lifetime.

According to some legends, the *bokor* would administer a powder mixture or sometimes a spell, either of which would subdue a person. The victim's heart and breathing rates would become greatly suppressed, and his or her body temperature would drop significantly to the point of appearing dead or, in some legends, actually dying. After the victim was pronounced dead and then buried, the *bokor* would exhume the body. The victim's memory would be gone, and that person would become a mindless drone used as the *bokor*'s personal slave.

Doomed to obey their *bokor* master, zombies could only understand basic commands. They had superior physical strength but a lack of responsiveness to stimuli, which made them resistant to pain and exhaustion—making them ideal for hard work. Some zombies were able to speak short, basic phrases, but their speech was said to be slurred. They communicated mostly with moans and groans. Despite the lack of physical damage to the body, the zombies in Haitian folklore were slow and clumsy, and they walked in a shuffle.

The original zombies had eyes in a fixed, expressionless stare, and their movements were repetitive and uncoordinated.

# ZOMBIES TRAVELED FROM AFRICA TO HAITI

Many features of Haitian legends of zombies can actually be traced back to African legends and spiritual beliefs. For several centuries, people in Africa were forcibly captured and shipped to the Americas, including the French colony of St. Domingue (modern-day Haiti), where they were sold as slaves. Many of these captured slaves brought their religious beliefs, including a West African belief system called Vodun, with them. The Vodou that developed in Haiti is an example of syncretism: it is a religion that incorporates and combines elements and symbolism from multiple religions, primarily Roman Catholicism and West African Vodun.

Vodou also contains elements of what is popularly called "black magic," which accounts for rituals such as the creation of zombies. It was this element that first captivated American audiences and helped mold the modern concept of Vodou that Hollywood still portrays—one that often bears little resemblance to the true religion.

Becoming a zombie would leave the victim in a dreamlike trance, with no awareness of his or her condition. These zombies were submissive and normally did not attack people unless commanded to do so by their *bokor*—something quite different from the zombies that many of us know on the big screen today.

There were always ways for zombies to break the *bokor*'s control over their bodies. If the *bokor* died, for example, the zombie would regain its freedom and be able to return to its family. In certain tales, the zombie's soul was kept in a vessel, such as a jar, by an incantation. If the vessel was broken, the zombie's soul could return to its body and the victim could regain his or her freedom. There are other zombie legends that stated that if a zombie were fed salt, it would regain its senses. Zombies freed in these ways still had a diminished mental state and were vulnerable to recapture. One final way that a zombie could be restored was through the divine intervention and mercy of a Vodou god—the only way that would fully restore a victim to his or her former state of health and vigor.

## SEEKING EXPLANATIONS

Reports of zombies were never taken very seriously by members of the scientific community or the general public outside Haiti despite some expeditions to investigate zombie folklore. In 1982, however, that would change and many would begin to look into scientific explanations for zombie lore.

After hearing reports of a man who claimed to have been a zombie and returned to his family twenty years later, a Canadian anthropologist named Wade Davis traveled to Haiti. Davis conducted several studies into the powders used by *bokor* (*bokor* is both the singular and plural version of the Haitian Creole word) and the lore surrounding zombies. Davis believed that plants containing psychoactive properties, or mind-altering effects, were responsible for most of the popular stories about zombies.

*Photographed is anthropologist Wade Davis in 1987, two years after his book* **The Serpent and the Rainbow** *was released. The work focused on Haitian zombie legends and gained widespread attention in the United States.*

After interviewing locals and testing samples, Davis discovered that *bokor* used mixtures of ground-up plant and animal parts that were unique in each case. Convinced that a drug was responsible for the zombie state of mind, Davis analyzed the available concoctions. He found that most of the powders included a varied amount of tetrodotoxin, a powerful poison derived from puffer fish that affects the nervous system. The toxin affects the brain, spinal cord, and nervous tissue in the victim's body. The dose would need to be specific for each potential victim. Too little of the toxin would not permanently establish a zombie-like state, but too much of the toxin would kill a victim completely.

Davis theorized that after a victim awoke from his or her presumed "death" and was exhumed by a *bokor*, the *bokor* would administer another drug to keep the person in a trance-like state and make it easy to control him or her. Davis furthermore suggested that the *bokor* would then give the victim regular doses of this drug to keep him or her in a zombie-like state. If the *bokor* stopped administering the drugs, the victim would no longer behave like a zombie. This theory explained how some "zombies" were able to regain their mental faculties after a *bokor*'s death and return to their families.

## SKEPTICISM

Skeptics questioned Davis's claims and pointed out the inconsistent amounts of the puffer fish toxin in alleged zombie powders. Others called stories about real-life zombies complete fabrications because of the lack of indisputable evidence. Davis defended his claims by offering reports from Japan—where puffer fish is a popular culinary dish—stating that people have been declared dead after having eaten puffer fish, only to later regain consciousness and completely recover. He further stated that the toxin was only one part of the powder by which *bokor* created zombies.

People continue to doubt the claims of Davis and others who defend the notion of the existence of real zombies. Whether zombies are a real possibility or nothing more than legend, there is no denying the appeal that zombies have over contemporary audiences. Some of today's zombies are quite different from the monster's Haitian roots. Films about zombies have become a popular obsession, feeding people's love of gore and horror. People's fear of zombies may have arisen like a corpse from the grave in colonial Haiti, but today's media has helped spread it worldwide. The film industry has converted people's innate fear into a captivating love of the carnage that zombies cause. The zombie craze has successfully infected millions worldwide and created an insatiable hunger for more undead action with no signs of being quarantined anytime soon.

# THE FIRST ZOMBIES HIT THE SCREEN

Zombie legends have been told for centuries but were not well known in the Western world until the early twentieth century. In terms of the big screen, many argue that the first zombie-like creature to make a theatrical appearance was that in the 1920 film *The Cabinet of Dr. Caligari*. In this German silent film, a zombie-like being behaved in a similar fashion to the way zombies were popularly depicted in Haitian tales. However, what the film showed was not technically a zombie (Dr. Caligari merely controlled his being as a sleepwalker and did not actually bring a human back from the dead). Nonetheless, it does represent one of the earliest appearances of a zombie-like creature in film. Tales brought from Haiti shortly after would help solidify the place of zombies in Hollywood culture.

# THE FIRST WAVE OF ZOMBIES HITS HOLLYWOOD

It was the release of such books as William Seabrook's *The Magic Island* (1929) and Zora Neale Hurston's *Tell My Horse* (1937) that brought authentic Haitian tales of zombies to an American audience (and took the entertainment industry by storm). In his book, Seabrook published a nonfiction account detailing his observations of Vodou and quoting reports from witnesses of alleged zombies. His travelogue of Haiti is widely believed to have roused fiction's love of zombies. By the time Hurston's work—which explored Haitian mythology and the folklore surrounding zombies—was released in 1937, zombies based on the Haitian legend had already begun appearing in films. Nonetheless, Hurston's book helped further fuel the public's fascination with the undead.

Soon after Seabrook's novel was released, movies began featuring zombies by name. In 1932, the first feature-length film to explicitly mention zombies, *White Zombie*, was released. Based on Seabrook's novel, the film starred Bela Lugosi as a main character. While Lugosi is best known for his role as Count Dracula, his portrayal of a shadowy sorcerer in *White Zombie* was just as captivating for audiences and made the film a Bela Lugosi classic. The film tells the story of a man who is obsessed with his friend's fiancée and becomes crazed by his love for her. He conspires with a sorcerer, Lugosi's character, to turn her into a zombie so that he can control her. The woman dies and is then resurrected as a zombie slave, but the man soon finds out that making deals with Lugosi comes with a price.

*In this scene from* **White Zombie, Annette Stone portrays Madge Bellamy, a woman cursed and turned into a zombie by a merciless sorcerer.**

Throughout the 1930s and '40s, love for zombies and other movies steeped in Haitian folklore spread across the world. Movies such as *Ouanga* (1936) and its remake *The Devil's Daughter* (1939) featured Vodou sorceresses as characters and Haitian plantations as settings (although they were, in fact, shot in Jamaica). *King of the Zombies* (1941) was also a popular film. The plot saw three characters survive a plane crash in the Caribbean and seek refuge in a large mansion. During their stay, however, they discover the mansion is haunted by zombies and also stumble upon a Vodou ritual in the basement.

In 1943, what is probably the second most popular zombie film of classic Hollywood was released: *I Walked with a Zombie*. A Canadian nurse named Betsy Connell (played by Frances Dee) is hired to care for a patient on a fictional Caribbean island. It is discovered, however, that the patient has been turned into a zombie, and elements of the Vodou religion come into play as they try to release the patient from her zombie state. Films such as the aforementioned helped zombies become a movie monster favorite, but later developments would take the zombie fad to a whole new level.

# ACQUIRING NEW TRAITS: MODERN MOVIE ZOMBIES

Early film adaptations of zombies generally remained faithful to Haitian folklore. They generally included elements of Vodou in their plots and often took place in the Caribbean, where zombies were alleged to appear. Later filmmakers, however, would adapt the concept of the living dead to other settings and deck zombies out with new qualities—often ones that had little relation to the original zombies of Haitian legend.

## SPEED

One of the biggest changes came in the Canadian film *Rabid* (1977). This movie gave audiences their first glimpse of zombies that were quick. Unlike the slow, lumbering zombies of Haitian legends and early Hollywood adaptations, many later films would make zombies fast. This movie features a woman who has been badly injured in a car accident. After receiving plastic and reconstructive surgery that contained infected tissue, she begins craving human flesh. Those who are bitten by her turn into zombies but retain their human speed.

In 1985, *The Return of the Living Dead* brought fast running zombies to the big screen once again with a storyline revolving around two clumsy employees at a medical supply warehouse who accidentally release a

**The Return of the Living Dead** *was one of the first American films to depict speedy zombies who ran instead of the slow, lumbering monsters of early zombie films.*

deadly gas. The fumes kill nearby residents, who then begin to rise from the dead as zombies. Famed director George A. Romero had depicted zombies who were aggressive toward humans in previous films, but Romero's zombies still moved in a slow shamble. In *Return of the Living Dead*, the employees spend all night fighting the speedy zombies before finally calling the military and telling them about the dilemma. In an attempt to destroy the zombies, the military drops a nuclear explosive on the town. As the movie ends, the audience is horrified to watch as the dead begin to rise again.

As audiences became less sensitive to zombie gore and more familiar with the lore, moviemakers began adapting the abilities, strength, and cleverness of zombies. Since the early 2000s, movies more often show zombies that are stronger and faster than their living human counterparts. Zombies' increased speed and strength is credited to their inability to feel pain or fatigue. Zombies can thus be classified into two groups: runners and walkers. Runners are fast and agile, while walkers shamble in groups.

Many zombie films in the 2000s also gave zombies a heightened sense of smell. In the television series *The Walking Dead* (which first aired in 2010), for example, zombies are capable of smelling humans as they hide. Humans often try to cover their scent with the blood or body of a zombie who has been successfully killed to avoid attack.

## ZOM COMS

Despite their overwhelming appearance in horror films, zombies have also become highly popular in another genre. Zom coms are a humorous twist on the standard scary zombie movie. Instead of being a true horror film, zom coms are comedies that feature zombies. In one popular film, *Shaun of the Dead* (2004), zombies retain the slow, lumbering movements of

**Shaun of the Dead** *took a more lighthearted approach to the zombie fad. In the early 2000s, filmmakers used comedy to take zombies beyond the horror genre.*
.

earlier zombies, but the film puts a comical spin on the idea of a zombie apocalypse. Another film, *Fido* (2006), is set in a 1950s-era community and comically portrays zombies as socially intelligent and compassionate creatures, allowing audiences to see zombies as tame and harmless rather than the bloodthirsty beasts that many movies make them out to be.

Other zom coms, such as *Zombieland* (2009), throw all these rules and notions aside and present viewers with a group of zombies who can think for themselves. A rag-tag group of zombies travel together across America in search of an amusement park and Twinkies. Many audiences like the different interpretations of what zombies would be like and capable of. This allows more leniencies for the producers, writers, and directors to create a zombie that better fits with their storyline.

19

## TURNING ZOMBIE

In the late 1950s and early 1960s, moviemakers began experimenting with the method in which people became zombies. Filmmakers no longer restricted themselves to Vodou rituals and began relying on new scientific ideas and ideas taken from science fiction films to resurrect the dead. Notably, in *Teenage Zombies* (1959), a mad scientist turns local teenagers into her personal zombie slaves using nerve gas. *Plan 9 from Outer Space* (1959) introduced aliens into zombie creation. In this film, aliens intend to create zombies in order to stop humanity from developing a type of sun-driven bomb later in the future. Its low-budget effects and awkward dialogue often earn this film a top spot on lists of the worst movies of all time, but footage of Bela Lugosi shot before his death and its memorable plot have made it a zombie classic.

*As this scene depicts,* Plan 9 from Outer Space *coupled zombie, alien, and vampire lore into one loosely connected plotline.*

In later films, the notion of an infection or biological cataclysm as the cause of zombification or the resurrection of the dead became commonplace. By using environmental agents such as infection as the cause for zombification, "zombiism" is easy to spread quickly through bites and even scratches. Because of their insatiable hunger, zombies are driven to relentlessly kill humans without pause. Because in these films anyone bitten or killed by a zombie will return as an undead creature him- or herself, zombies can quickly grow into a large group of flesh-eating monsters that can easily overpower humans. Biological sources of zombiism allow for films to exploit the possibility of the undead accumulating and quickly outnumbering living humans.

## OTHER CHANGES IN THE ZOMBIE GENRE

Early movie zombies tended to be afraid of fire and bright lights. Humans in these films could use torches to slow down zombies and gain more time to either escape or find a weapon to defend themselves. In the movie *Planet Terror* (2007), however, the zombies were attracted to fire. A throwback to the low-budget films of the 1970s, *Planet Terror* depicts thousands of zombies created by an experimental bioweapon. In *The Walking Dead* television series, the zombies are similarly attracted to a house fire by the light and even from the smoke from a distance.

# THE CREATOR OF A MODERN MONSTER

We've already seen that, in Haitian legends, zombies were mild-mannered and slow moving, and lacked the ability to think or make decisions for themselves. They followed their *bokor*'s orders and posed little threat to other humans. Early moviemakers stuck to that script, but later filmmakers realized that greater eminent danger would attract more viewers. Changes in the adaptation of zombies from Caribbean legends to the big screen were inevitable. However, contemporary moviegoers may not realize that most of the zombie attributes seen in American zombie films today all came from one director's mind.

## THE MAKING OF THE MODERN ZOMBIE

Credited with creating the modern zombie, George A. Romero started his career shooting commercials and short films with his friends in Pittsburgh, Pennsylvania. In the 1960s, they established

Image Ten Productions, a production company, and initially scraped together about $6,000 (the total cost would end up being about $114,000) to create what would become one of the most celebrated American horror films of all time: *Night of the Living Dead* (1968). The script was written by Romero along with Image Ten Productions cofounder John Russo, but the black-and-white film developed what was truly Romero's vision of the undead.

*American film director George A. Romero, shown here in 1980, is widely known as the father of the modern movie zombie.*

*Night of the Living Dead* quickly became a cult classic and earned far more money than it had cost to shoot it (about $12–15 million in its first decade). Part of its success was a result of the excessive amount of gore that had not been present in previous horror films. Yet, it was not just the violence that skyrocketed the film's success; the solidly written storyline emphasized the

23

# BEYOND ZOMBIES: ROMERO'S ROOTS

George A. Romero was born on February 4, 1940, in New York City, New York. Romero lived in New York until he left to attend Carnegie Mellon University in Pittsburgh, Pennsylvania, from which he graduated in 1960. Romero decided to stay in Pennsylvania after college, and after establishing a production company with his friends in Pittsburgh, he filmed nearly all of his works there. First, of course, was the 1968 cult classic *Night of the Living Dead*.

Romero's subsequent films were not as popular as his first, but each was notable in its own way. Despite being conceptually similar to *Night of the Living Dead*, *The Crazies* (1973) was not, in fact, a zombie film. In this movie, citizens of a small Pennsylvania town are overrun by the victims of a manmade virus that causes death and insanity to those infected. The military then arrives and attempts to contain the situation. The feral and violent nature of those infected resembles zombies' aggressive nature, but the infected citizens are not dead nor are they cannibalistic.

Romero's attempts at horror films outside of the zombie genre were not as acclaimed as his zombie-related works. Audiences were not as receptive to his more low-key films outside of the zombie genre. In 1978, he returned to zombie films with *Dawn of the Dead*. Romero's adaptations to the zombie genre would forever change what audiences expected of zombies.

torment, confusion, and fear of the cast of humans trapped in a house while avoiding a zombie attack.

The film centers on a distraught woman, Barbra, who flees a cemetery after her brother, Johnny, is attacked and killed by an undead corpse. A nearby man named Ben takes Barbra, and the two barricade themselves in a house that they believe to be empty before encountering a few others strangers hiding out in the basement. The group of survivors contemplates the cause of the reanimation of the recently dead, but the film never really specifies a true cause. Most of Romero's other works hold to this practice, allowing the audience members to speculate on its frightening cause. The film is notable for the dynamic relationships that develop among the strangers holed up together—relationships that change from fear to mutual protection.

Barbra and Ben initially believe that they are safe in the house where they sought refuge, but they later learn that the daughter of the family hiding in the basement has been bitten. They stitch together a plan for getting gasoline from a nearby gas pump in order to fill up a truck and escape the zombie attack. However, panic, personal tensions, and ravenous walking corpses add to the terror and ultimate unlikeness of Romero's cast surviving the night.

## HOW *NIGHT OF THE LIVING DEAD* CHANGED ZOMBIES

In *Night of the Living Dead*, there are no *bokor* or magic potions. Instead, anyone who is bitten by a zombie will become a zombie him- or herself, and the only way to stop a zombie is to destroy its brain. The concept of killing a zombie by destroying its brain has been adopted by Hollywood as the favorite and often only way to stop a zombie. Many of Romero's others additions and notions about the undead laid the framework for the zombie films that followed.

In *Night of the Living Dead*, Romero's zombies crave human flesh and will stop at nothing to get it. They are still slow and shamble like the zombies of Haitian lore (it was later filmmakers in the late 1970s and early 1980s who introduced the new elements of speed and superb physical abilities to zombies), but because zombiism is so contagious in Romero's film, they soon outnumber the living. Romero's changes to the idea of the living dead—that they are aggressive toward humans and that their bites turn victims into new zombies—became the single most influential development in turning zombies on the big screen into what they've since become. The success of Romero's first film grossed over $18 million worldwide and led to Romero's career as a director—a career that would forever evolve America's love for zombies.

## ROMERO RISES AGAIN

Romero revisited the zombie genre in 1978, and his work once again captivated audiences' attention. With *Dawn of the Dead*, Romero fans once again lavished in the gore and the struggles of a group of humans left to fend for themselves as a plague of zombies attack.

*Dawn of the Dead* follows four strangers who take refuge in a vacant shopping mall when faced with oncoming zombies.

*This scene from* **Dawn of the Dead** *depicts zombies breaching the safety of the mall where survivors had barricaded themselves.* **Dawn of the Dead** *was Romero's most successful film.*

They lock down the mall and kill the few zombies that were already inside the building. The survivors decide to stay in the mall and try to carry on with their lives there. Soon after, however, personal tensions begin to weigh on the group as a large gang of bikers discovers the mall. Safe and protected from the zombies outside, the mall is also the perfect hideout for the bikers, and they invade. The protagonists must then fight off both the deadly bandit-bikers and the flesh-eating zombies.

27

*Dawn of the Dead* cost about $650,000 to make. The profits more than made up for the costs with estimates of it having grossed $55 million worldwide. Because of its widespread success, *Dawn of the Dead* was ranked on Entertainment Weekly's Top 50 Cult Films in 2003. The success of the movie also initialized a remake in 2004.

Romero's films consistently have the theme of a small group of humans trying to survive and barricade themselves as an ever-growing horde of zombies threatens to destroy everyone. Each film's group must collaborate and develop a hasty escape plan. By highlighting the struggles of a small, often diverse group, Romero helps viewers connect to the characters more closely. Considerable time is spent on character development, a technique that makes viewers grow more attached to the protagonists and hope for their survival. When the inevitable death of a character occurs, viewers are more horrified and distraught by the catastrophe.

## DAY OF THE DEAD AND ROMERO'S LATER WORKS

Romero's films exemplified the concept of undead corpses lumbering around, driven by the compulsive need to kill the living. His well-structured plots draw in audiences and capture the popular imagination. However, by the late 1980s, Romero's career began to decline. The release of *Day of the Dead* (1985), the third film in his *Dead* series, brought a decline in his success.

*Day of the Dead* featured a small group of scientists and military personnel who dwell in an underground bunker as zombies ravage the world above them. Desperate for a cure, they conduct barbaric and gruesome experiments on the undead. It is a race against death and time as zombies attempt to infiltrate the bunker and take over the facility.

*Day of the Dead* was derided by critics and did not gross much in the box office. Romero's earlier films received much higher praise from critics than his later works. Much to the dismay of Romero's fans, he was unable to overcome the success of

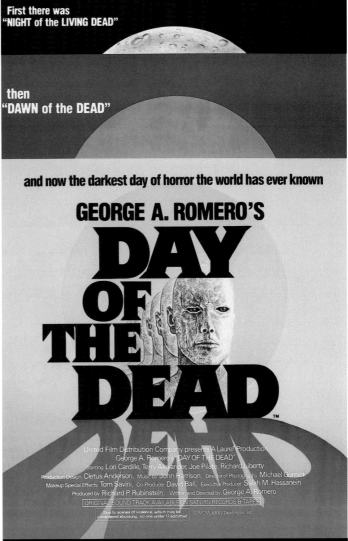

First there was
"NIGHT of the LIVING DEAD"

then
"DAWN of the DEAD"

and now the darkest day of horror the world has ever known

GEORGE A. ROMERO'S

DAY OF THE DEAD

United Film Distribution Company presents A Laurel Production
George A. Romero's "DAY OF THE DEAD"
Starring Lori Cardille, Terry Alexander, Joe Pilato, Richard Liberty
Production Design Cletus Anderson, Music by John Harrison, Director of Photography Michael Gornick
Makeup Special Effects Tom Savini, Co-Producer David Ball, Executive Producer Salah M. Hassanein
Produced by Richard P. Rubinstein, Written and Directed by George A. Romero
ORIGINAL SOUND TRACK AVAILABLE ON SATURN RECORDS & TAPES
Due to scenes of violence, which may be considered shocking, no one under 17 admitted. © MCMLXXXV Dead Films Inc.

*Romero's third zombie film,* **Day of the Dead,** *was the lowest grossing film in the* **Dead** *trilogy. Nonetheless, it gained a cult following among Romero fans in the decades following its release.*

his first films, and he did not work much after his final few box office failures. However, in 2005, Romero released *Land of the Dead*, which renewed his status as an authority of zombie culture.

In *Land of the Dead*, Romero revisited the zombie apocalypse with a slightly different approach. The surviving humans in this film build a walled-in city to safely live out their lives separate from those who have been turned into zombies. However, as time progresses, the zombies in this film become increasingly advanced and eventually invade the city. Audiences were excited about Romero's return to the big screen in a new decade. *Land of the Dead* topped the box-office in its first week of release.

## STRONG MINORITY ROLES

From the beginning, Romero's production company, Image Ten Productions, made it common practice to hire people who had a hard time finding work. In the 1960s, minorities and women in particular had a tough time finding work. The civil rights movement was at its peak, and minorities and women in the United States were demanding greater rights.

When Romero and his production team shot *Night of the Living Dead*, they auditioned several people, but when Duane Jones (an African American actor) tried out for the role of Ben, they gave him the part. Despite what viewers at the time might have thought about casting an African American as the lead hero, Romero knew he had found the perfect protagonist in

Jones. Romero did not look at Jones's race as a contributing factor when casting him, nor did he intend to change the script in any way either. Romero's team did eventually rewrite some of the dialogue in the script at Jones's request.

Jones's role was originally written to portray Ben as a lower-class and undereducated man. However, Jones himself was highly educated and even spoke multiple languages. Jones felt that Ben should have better grammar and vocabulary than the original script presented. Romero agreed. The result was

*Ben and Barbra, the main characters in* **Night of the Living Dead**, *are shown here taking refuge from a zombie horde inside a country house. Romero was known for casting minorities and women and depicting them as strong protagonists.*

a more natural and intense character—one that challenged expectations for a black protagonist.

Romero also came to depict women as more resourceful than in other films of the time. However, that was not initially the case. *Night of the Living Dead* portrays women as subdued and timid. Barbra and other female characters in the film have meeker manners than their male counterparts. As his film lineage progressed, Romero began writing his female characters to be more outspoken and educated—a reflection of changes in the public's attitudes. These later characters expressed more complex views of women and allowed women to become their own heroes and save themselves. In *Dawn of the Dead*, for example, main character Francine Parker is both pregnant and a working professional. She also survives over two of her fellow male counterparts and is responsible for flying the getaway helicopter to escape the zombie invasion.

Another casting technique of Romero's is the use of a blend of professional and amateur actors. This has contributed to the success of his films because it provides more believable characters in the depiction of a crisis such as a zombie outbreak. While he was not the first to produce a zombie film, he will forever be known as the director who created the modern movie monster that is the zombie we all know and fear.

# THE ZOMBIE PHENOMENON

Since 2000, there has been a resurgence in the popularity of zombies in film and other media. The zombie craze has infected almost every media format across the globe. Furthermore, zombies are crossing genres—meaning zombies from novels, comic books, and video game formats have found their way to the big screen. Countless reanimated corpses shamble across televisions in spin-offs and sequels, invading pop culture at an unstoppable rate. Particularly popular is the idea of a zombie apocalypse, or the destruction of modern society by the undead.

## ZOMBIE NOVELS HIT THE BIG SCREEN

With the renewed growth of the zombie trend have come zombie novels—as well as film adaptations of those novels. Perhaps the best-known zombie novels to translate to film are *World War Z*, *Autumn*, and *Pride and Prejudice and Zombies*. Author Max

Brooks has written several zombie novels, but his most popular yet, *World War Z*, made it to theaters in 2013. Generally positively reviewed by critics, *World War Z* follows a former United Nations employee as he travels across the world to find a cure for the zombie pandemic. Multiple times the characters in this film barely escape rampaging zombies in this action-packed film that reels the audience in and keeps them on the edge of their seats.

*Autumn* (2009) was based on a series of novels by David Moody. Although the books were given rave reviews, the film

*The high-action pace of the novel* World War Z *made it a perfect text to be reinvented for audiences through film.*

version was not as well received. It tells the story of a spreading virus that kills billions of humans within minutes. After the few survivors process the initial shock, the dead begin to rise again. The longer the zombies are revived, the more their senses and basic faculties return to them, making them increasingly dangerous.

*Pride and Prejudice and Zombies* puts a different twist on the classic novel *Pride and Prejudice* by Jane Austen. Written by Seth Grahame-Smith, this parody novel follows

**Pride and Prejudice and Zombies** *was one of the most popular books in the monster mash-up genre. In 2009, plans were announced to take the novel to the big screen.*

the classic character Elizabeth Bennet as she battles insatiable zombies, all the while trying to win Mr. Darcy's love. In 2009, it was announced that a film adaptation of the movie would be made and hype for the American zom com romance film was immense. And it's no surprise why! Zombies have taken over

## ZOMBIES TAKE THE SMALL SCREEN, TOO

Novels are not the only zombie literature to get a visual treatment. Zombie-based graphic novels and comic books have also found their way onto the small screen—television. The most popular zombie comic book conversion is inarguably *The Walking Dead* series.

Picked up by the cable television channel AMC in 2010, *The Walking Dead* follows a group of survivors as they band together to stay alive. The show highlights both the external threats of being eaten by zombies or killed at the hands of the living and the inner struggle that the survivors face as they try desperately not to lose what humanity they have left. In search of a safe haven, the group of protagonists travels across America as they avoid being killed by shuffling hordes of hungry zombies, or "walkers," as the show calls them. This post-apocalyptic horror series focuses primarily on the dramas and dilemmas the group faces as they try to survive and adjust to the world now that it is filled with ravenous zombies and hostile humans.

*AMC's* **The Walking Dead** *series has gained huge success in the zombie genre. It follows a group of humans who must survive bands of "walkers," or zombies.*

The AMC hit show was an immediate success

and quickly amassed an ever-growing fan base. The success of the series even led to an after show, *Talking Dead*, which began airing immediately after each night's episode during season two of *The Walking Dead* (2011–2012).

both horror and comedy—and excelled at the box office while they're at it.

## VIDEO GAME ZOMBIES

Video games are another medium that has been overrun by zombies and, as with zombie novels and comic books, taken to the big screen. Several popular zombie video games have been adapted into film format. *The House of the Dead*, for example, was a popular light gun arcade game published by Sega in 1996. In 2003, it was adapted into the horror film *House of the Dead*, directed by Uwe Boll. Yet, the inarguably most successful video game–movie franchise of all time has been *Resident Evil*. In just five film adaptions, the *Resident Evil* series grossed over $900 million at the box office, with plans to continue onward with additional releases and adaptations.

The *Resident Evil* storyline revolves around Alice, who is an employee of the fictional Umbrella Corporation at the time when a bio-weapon known as the t-Virus is released inside a top-secret laboratory. The t-Virus infects the entire staff, initially killing all inside the laboratory. Those infected, however, do not stay dead. Those humans (and animals, too) who contract the virus return as cannibalistic zombies. When the Special

Tactics and Rescue Service (STARS) team is called to investigate what is believed to be a series of homicides, it accidentally releases the creatures—and the virus they carry—into the outside world. Once the nearby Raccoon City, a fictional city in the video game and film series, is exposed to the t-Virus, the zombie apocalypse sweeps across the world, and it is up to Alice to try to stop it.

# OUR FASCINATION WITH ZOMBIES

The public's love of zombies stems from a blend of fascination and fear. The idea of the zombie acknowledges both our curiosity about the afterlife and our fears of the possible effects of a mass bio-hazardous event or infectious outbreak. Anthrax, SARS, and Ebola are just a few of the bacterial and viral infections that have caused worldwide panic at the first signs of their outbreak. As any good horror film genre seeks to do, contemporary zombie movies play on people's fears of biochemical weapons and the possibility of an outbreak. Classic zombie films appeal to our intrigue about what comes after death.

Zombie films play on viewers' personal fears as a way of increasing the anxiety and believability of a plot. Zombie movies are often set in seemingly normal, realistic towns—one with which the audience is familiar—and they cast relatable characters to make the plot more convincing. Survivors must rely on each other for protection and assistance, a tactic that ultimately plays on people's fears of a collapsed society. While free from

zombies, the survivors' safe haven is often ultimately plagued instead by issues that arise among the living because of distress and panic. Zombie films rely on this blend of fears—fear of despair and desolation, of mass-scaled infection, of hordes of ravenous cannibals, and of hostile vigilantes—to intrigue the audience and bring them back to the theater.

*With zombie popularity on the rise, "zombie walks" have sprung up across the globe. During this 2014 walk in Berlin, Germany, over 150 participants dressed as zombies to gather in a "zombie walk" flash mob.*

While scientists and governments concur that a zombie apocalypse is not a real possibility any time soon, zombies have still taken over our world at a ravenous pace, one horror flick at a time. They strike a chord with many of our deepest fears in a globalized society with nuclear weapons, unchecked scientific developments, and millions of passengers flying worldwide each day. These unanswered fears raise the pulse and pump adrenaline through the bloodstream, making zombies some of today's greatest movie monsters.

# FILMOGRAPHY

**The Cabinet of Dr. Caligari** (1920)
Director: Robert Wiene
Actors: Werner Krauss, Conrad Veidt, and Friedrich Fehér

**White Zombie** (1932)
Director: Victor Halperin
Actors: Bela Lugosi and Madge Bellamy

**The Devil's Daughter** (1939)
Director: Arthur H. Leonard
Actors: Nina Mae McKinney, Jack Carter, and Ida James

**King of the Zombies** (1941)
Director: Jean Yarbrough
Actors: Dick Purcell and Joan Woodbury

**I Walked with a Zombie** (1943)
Director: Jacques Tourneur
Actors: Frances Dee and Tom Conway

**Plan 9 from Outer Space** (1959)
Director: Edward D. Wood Jr.
Actors: Gregory Walcott, Tom Keene, and Mona McKinnon

**Teenage Zombies** (1959)
Director: Jerry Warren
Actors: Katherine Victor and Don Sullivan

**Night of the Living Dead** (1968)
Director: George A. Romero
Actors: Duane Jones and Judith O'Dea

**Rabid** (1977)
Director: David Cronenberg
Actors: Marilyn Chambers and Frank Moore

**Dawn of the Dead** (1978)
Director: George A. Romero
Actors: David Emge, Ken Foree, and Scott H. Reiniger

**Day of the Dead (1985)**
Director: George A. Romero
Actors: Lori Cardille and Terry Alexander

**Return of the Living Dead (1985)**
Director: Dan O'Bannon
Actors: Clu Gulager and James Karen

**28 Days Later (2002)**
Director: Danny Boyle
Actors: Cillian Murphy and Naomie Harris

**Resident Evil (2002)**
Director: Paul W. S. Anderson
Actors: Milla Jovovich, Michelle Rodriguez, and Ryan McCluskey

**Shaun of the Dead (2004)**
Director: Edgar Wright
Actors: Simon Pegg, Nick Frost, and Kate Ashfield

**Land of the Dead (2005)**
Director: George A. Romero
Actors: John Leguizamo and Asia Argento

**Fido (2006)**
Director: Andrew Currie
Actors: Kesun Loder and Billy Connolly

**Planet Terror (2007)**
Director: Robert Rodriguez
Actors: Rose McGowan and Freddy Rodriguez

**28 Weeks Later (2007)**
Director: Juan Carlos Fresnadillo
Actors: Jeremy Renner and Rose Byrne

**Zombieland (2009)**
Director: Ruben Fleischer
Actors: Jesse Eisenberg, Emma Stone, and Woody Harrelson

**World War Z (2013)**
Director: Marc Forster
Actors: Brad Pitt, Mireille Enos, and Daniella Kertesz

# GLOSSARY

**AMASS** To gather or collect in great quantities.

*BOKOR* A voodoo priest or other practitioner of black magic.

**CATACLYSM** A large-scale and violent event in the natural world.

**CONCOCTION** Something prepared or made by combining ingredients.

**DYNAMIC** Characterized by constant change, activity, or progress.

**INSATIABLE** Incapable of being satisfied or appeased.

**LENIENCY** Tolerance or mercy beyond expectations.

**PROTAGONIST** The leading character or hero of a work of literature or film.

**QUARANTINE** Forced detention or isolation for the sake of preventing the spread of disease.

**RAVENOUS** Insatiably hungry and devouring large amounts of food.

**REANIMATE** To restore to life or resuscitate.

**SYNCRETISM** The attempted union of elements pertaining to different religions.

**TETRODOTOXIN** A neurotoxin that occurs in puffer fish, the ingestion of which causes heart failure or asphyxiation.

**TRAVELOGUE** A movie, book, or other form of documents about the places visited and experiences of a traveler.

**ZOMBIISM** The condition or state of being a zombie.

# FOR MORE INFORMATION

Centers for Disease Control and Prevention

1600 Clifton Road

Atlanta, GA 30329

(800) 232-4636

Website: http://www.cdc.gov

The Centers for Disease Control and Prevention (CDC) teaches the public about emergency preparedness and has capitalized on the idea of the zombie apocalypse by providing a preparedness checklist for any disaster—including zombie attacks.

National Film Board of Canada (NFB)

P.O. Box 6100

Station Centre-ville

Montreal, QC H3C 3H5

Canada

Website: http://www.nfb.ca

The NFB is the premier public producer and distributor of film in Canada.

STEM Behind Hollywood

P.O. Box 660199

Dallas, TX 75266

(800) 842-2737

Website: http://education.ti.com/en/us/stem-hollywood

STEM Behind Hollywood was created to get students excited about the real-world science, technology, engineering, and mathematics (STEM) careers that help make Hollywood magic—including on-screen monsters.

Zombie Research Society

E-mail: Mogk@ZRS.me

Website: http://zombieresearchsociety.com

Zombie Research Society (ZRS) is dedicated to the history of zombies as well as the cultural and scientific study of the undead. Active members include authors, academics, and zombie enthusiasts committed to real-life research of the undead.

Zombie Squad, Inc.

P.O. Box 63124

St. Louis, MO 63163

(888) 495-4052

Website: https://www.zombiehunters.org

Zombie Squad is a nonprofit community service and disaster preparedness organization that uses the metaphor of a "Zombie Apocalypse" for any natural or man-made disaster.

# WEBSITES

Because of the changing nature of Internet links, Rosen Publishing has developed an online list of websites related to the subject of this book. This site is updated regularly. Please use this link to access the list:

http://www.rosenlinks.com/GMM/Zomb

# FOR FURTHER READING

Austin, John. *So Now You're a Zombie: A Handbook for the Newly Undead*. Chicago, IL: Chicago Review, 2010.

Bailey, Diane. *Zombies in America*. New York, NY: Rosen Publishing Group, 2012.

Dakota, Heather, and Ali Castro. *Zombie Apocalypse Survival Guide*. New York, NY: Scholastic, 2014.

Johnson, Rebecca. *Zombie Makers: True Stories of Nature's Undead*. Minneapolis, MN: Millbrook Press, 2012.

Kane, Joe. *Night of the Living Dead: Behind the Scenes of the Most Terrifying Zombie Movie Ever*. New York, NY: Citadel, 2010.

Kay, Glenn. *Zombie Movies: The Ultimate Guide*. Chicago, IL: Chicago Review Press, 2012.

Kloepfer, John. *The Zombie Chasers, 1*. New York, NY: HarperCollins, 2011.

Marion, Isaac. *Warm Bodies: A Novel*. New York, NY: Atria, 2011.

Mogk, Matt. *Everything You Ever Wanted to Know About Zombies*. New York, NY: Gallery, 2011.

Montandon, Mac. *Proper Care and Feeding of Zombies: A Completely Scientific Guide to the Lives of the Undead*. Hoboken, NJ: Wiley, 2010.

Owens, Ruth. *Zombies and Other Walking Dead* (Not Near Normal: The Paranormal). New York, NY: Bearport Publishing, 2013.

Pearlman, Robb. *101 Ways to Kill a Zombie*. Milford, CT: Universe, 2013.

Russell, Jamie. *Book of the Dead: The Complete History of Zombie Cinema*. London, England: Titan Books, 2014.

Shone, Rob. *Zombies: Tales of the Living Dead*. New York, NY: Rosen Publishing Group, 2011.

Troupe, Thomas Kingsley, and Francesca Dafne Vignaga. *The Legend of the Zombie*. Mankato, MN: Picture Window, 2012.

# BIBLIOGRAPHY

Encylopedia Britannica. "The Magic Island (work by Seabrook)." Retrieved November 11, 2014 (http://www.britannica.com).

Ferguson, James. "Haiti." Encyclopædia Britannica. Retrieved November 11, 2014 (http://www.britannica.com).

IMDb. "Dawn of the Dead." Retrieved November 11, 2014 (http://www.imdb.com/title/tt0077402/?ref_=nmbio_mbio).

IMDb. "George A. Romero: Biography." Retrieved November 11, 2014 (http://www.imdb.com/name/nm0001681/bio?ref_=nm_ov_bio_sm).

IMDb. "Night of the Living Dead." Retrieved November 11, 2014 (http://www.imdb.com/title/tt0063350/?ref_=nmbio_mbio).

IMDb. "White Zombie." Retrieved November 11, 2014 (http://www.imdb.com/title/tt0023694/synopsis?ref_=ttpl_pl_syn).

Lee, Roberts. "Zombie Movie History." Retrieved November 11, 2014 (http://www.best-horror-movies.com/zombie-movie-history).

McAlister, Elizabeth. "Slaves, Cannibals, and Infected Hyper-Whites: The Race and Religion of Zombies." WesScholar. Retrieved November 11, 2014 (http://wesscholar.wesleyan.edu).

Mysterious Universe. "The Mysterious Real Zombies of Haiti." Retrieved November 11, 2014 (http://mysteriousuniverse.org).

The Society Pages. "The Origin of Zombies." Retrieved November 11, 2014 (http://thesocietypages.org).

University of Michigan. "Zombie History and Haitian Folklore." Retrieved November 11, 2014 (http://www.umich.edu/~engl415/zombies/zombie.html).

The Wrap. "How Casting a Black Actor Changed 'Night of the Living Dead.'" The Wrap. Retrieved November 11, 2014 (http://www.thewrap.com).

# INDEX

## ABOUT THE AUTHOR

Kathryn Morgan is an author of monster fiction with a love of all things supernatural. She has been writing since 2012 and has published four books thus far. Her research into zombie folklore has piqued her interests of the undead even further, which may spark many more books to come.

## PHOTO CREDITS

Cover, p. 19 © AF Archive/Alamy; pp. 5, 36 Gene Page/©AMC/ courtesy Everett Collection; p. 6 7 Continents History/Everett Collection; pp. 10, 15 courtesy Everett Collection; pp. 17, 29 © Everett Collection/Alamy; p. 20 © Ronald Grant Archive/ Alamy; p. 23 Michael Ochs Archives/Getty Images; p. 27 © Photos 12/Alamy; p. 31 © IMAGE TEN/Ronald Grant Archive/ Mary Evans/Alamy; p. 34 © Moviestore Collection Ltd/Alamy; p. 35 © AP Images; p. 39 Target Presse Agentur Gmbh/Getty Images; pp. 40–41 Andrey_Kuzmin/Shutterstock.com; interior pages banners and backgrounds Nik Merkulov/Shutterstock .com, Apostrophe/Shutterstock.com.

Designer: Brian Garvey